An Insider's Guide to
SOFTBALL

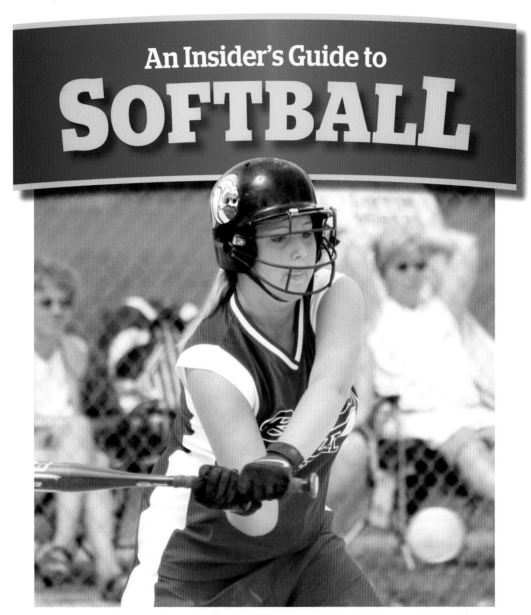

JAYNE BAKER AND ADAM B. HOFSTETTER

rosen publishing's
rosen
central®

NEW YORK

Published in 2015 by The Rosen Publishing Group, Inc.
29 East 21st Street, New York, NY 10010

First Edition

Library of Congress Cataloging-in-Publication Data

Baker, Jayne.
An insider's guide to softball/by Jayne Baker and Adam B. Hofstetter.
    pages cm.—(Sports tips, techniques, and strategies)
Includes bibliographic references and index.
ISBN 978-1-4777-8587-4 (library binding)—ISBN 978-1-4777-8588-1 (pbk.)—
ISBN 978-1-4777-8590-4 (6-pack)
1. Softball—Juvenile literature. I. Title.
GV881.15 B35 2015
796.357—d23

Manufactured in Malaysia

Metric Conversion Chart			
1 inch	2.54 centimeters 25.4 millimeters	1 cup	250 milliliters
1 foot	30.48 centimeters	1 ounce	28 grams
1 yard	.914 meters	1 fluid ounce	30 milliliters
1 square foot	.093 square meters	1 teaspoon	5 milliliters
1 square mile	2.59 square kilometers	1 tablespoon	15 milliliters
1 ton	.907 metric tons	1 quart	.946 liters
1 pound	454 grams	355 degrees F	180 degrees C
1 mile	1.609 kilometers		

Contents

CHAPTER 1

Softball: A History

Softball was played as an Olympic sport for the first time at the 1996 Summer Games in Atlanta, Georgia. It's probably a safe bet that nobody there thought about Thanksgiving. But if Thanksgiving Day in 1887 had gone a bit differently, softball might not exist.

That day, a group of alumni from Yale and Harvard gathered at the Farragut Boat Club in Chicago, Illinois. They were there to hear the score of a football game being played between the two universities. While celebrating the Yale victory, someone tossed a boxing glove at one of the Harvard folks. He, in turn, picked up a stick and swatted the glove back over the Yale fan's head. George Hancock, a reporter from the Chicago Board of Trade, saw what happened. Inspired by the boxing glove, Hancock imagined a fun, indoor version of baseball that could be played during the cold Chicago winters. Using the boxing glove's strings, he tied it into a ball. The first ever game of softball was played that very night, with chalk baselines and a broomstick handle for a bat.

The 1897 Chicago softball team was one of the earliest full-fledged teams to play formal softball.

Hancock and other members of the Farragut Boat Club established a few rules over the next week. Hancock developed a ball with a 16-inch circumference and a small bat. Because the ball was soft, players did not wear mitts as in baseball. The game quickly spread all over Chicago.

In 1889, Hancock issued the first softball rule book. Hancock's game wasn't called softball just yet. It was simply called "indoor baseball." When the game achieved national popularity in the 1890s, it was known as "kitten league ball" or "kitten ball," named after one of the first teams to play it.

George Hancock, *(above)*, invented the game of softball. He wrote its first rule book and is often referred to as the father of softball.

In 1895, a fireman named Lewis Rober, Sr., from Minneapolis, Minnesota, took the game outdoors. He set up a field in a vacant lot near his firehouse so that his fellow firemen could get some exercise. Rober used a 12-inch ball, which eventually became the standard worldwide.

Over the years, the game was also called "diamond ball," "pumpkin ball," and "mush ball." The game was finally named "softball" in 1926, when Walter Hakanson of the YMCA of Denver, Colorado, suggested it to the International Joint Rules Committee.

12 inches

Today, the standard size of a softball is 12 inches.

Softball Gains in Popularity

The game's rules took just as long to be standardized as the ball did. Softball leagues were springing up quickly, and each one fashioned its own set of rules to fit the players and the circumstances. Some leagues preferred the fast-pitch game, while others preferred slow-pitch softball. Some groups allowed teams to use a tenth fielder, while others followed traditional baseball rules and allowed only nine fielders. What the sport needed was a national governing body to organize teams and direct the growth of the sport.

In 1933, the first national amateur softball tournament was held. Organizers wisely scheduled the tournament as part of the Chicago World's Fair, which helped introduce the game to people from all over the country and the world. Champions were crowned in a women's division and in men's fast-pitch and slow-pitch. The success of the tournament finally led to the founding of the Amateur Softball Association (ASA) later that year. The first widely accepted rule book was produced by this group. Apart from this, the ASA also organized fair

Major General Gilbert Cheves *(left)* and Major General Claire Chennault *(right)* open a softball game in China in 1945 with a custom often observed in America.

and consistent tournaments around the country. The standardization of the rules facilitated the growth of the sport. Historians estimate that as many as five million people around the world were playing organized softball by the end of the 1930s.

During World War II (1941–1945), softball spread internationally, as American soldiers played and taught the game wherever they were stationed. The game took another big leap forward in 1946, with the establishment of the U.S. National Fastball League.

The week of July 22–28, 1951, was declared National Softball Week, and the following year saw the founding of the International Softball Federation (ISF). The ISF is now the universal governing body for the sport.

The King's Court

In the spring of 1946, 21-year-old Eddie Feigner was pitching for a local fast-pitch team in Pendleton, Oregon. After walloping yet another

opposing team, Feigner was heckled by some of the losing players. In response, he boasted, "I would play you with only my catcher, but you would walk us both." On a dare, the opposing manager challenged Feigner to play against his nine-man squad with only four players: pitcher, catcher, first baseman, and shortstop. Feigner and his three teammates took them up on the challenge.

Eddie "The King" Feigner was famous for pitching behind his back.

(*continued on page 8*)

(*continued from page 7*)

Feigner and his team decided to call themselves "The King and His Court." Incredibly, they won their first four-on-nine game by a score of 7–0. Eddie "The King" Feigner pitched a perfect game, striking out nineteen of the twenty-one batters in the seven-inning game.

Before long, Feigner and his team were touring all over the world. The King wowed fans and hitters with a fast-ball that was once clocked at 104 miles per hour. In 1967, in an exhibition at Dodger Stadium, Feigner struck out six baseball legends, including Willie Mays, Brooks Robinson, and Roberto Clemente, all in a row!

The King and His Court dominated so thoroughly that they started concentrating more on amusing the fans with trick plays and other high jinks. For parts of each game, Feigner would pitch behind his back, between his legs, blindfolded, from second base, or even from centerfield.

In 2006, at the age of eighty-one, the King finally retired after his sixty-first year of touring the world with his Court. He died from respiratory complications a year later, on February 9, 2007.

Softball Makes a Global Impact

In 1965, women's softball teams from five countries competed in Australia in the game's first World Championship. The host team took home the title. The first men's World Championship was held in Mexico the following year, with the U.S. men's team prevailing. Softball continued to expand, adding junior men's and junior women's world championships in 1981, and the Men's World Slow Pitch Championship in 1987. By then, tens of millions of people around the world were playing softball in Little Leagues, in weekend pickup games, and in major college athletic programs. The introduction of women's fast-pitch softball at the Summer Olympics in Atlanta, Georgia, in 1996, is evidence of the sport's growing popularity. That year, the fast-pitched game gained immense popularity and participation when the women's U.S. team won their first Olympic gold medal. The U.S. Women's National Team won Olympic gold again in both 2000 and 2004. Unfortunately, in July 2005, the International Olympic Committee made the decision to eliminate softball (and baseball) from the Olympics, beginning with the 2012 Games. Although a lot of effort was put into trying to get the game reinstated for the 2016, 2020 and 2024 Olympics, softball lost the vote to wrestling in September 2013.

Softball has become more popular among women than men.
Pictured above are players from Penn State in a game against Texas.

CHAPTER 2

The Game

Softball is played by all types of people at every level of competition. Players at the highest levels are great athletes. However, you don't have to be in top shape to enjoy the game. Boys and girls as young as five or six years old play, as do adults well past retirement age.

Despite its origins as an indoor game, softball is now almost always played outdoors. It can be played all year-round in warmer climates, but the season is usually limited to spring and summer in colder areas. (Truly dedicated players may join "frostbite" leagues, which play games well into the fall.) For an organized game, a softball or baseball field is ideal. For an informal game, however, all you need is a ball, a bat, mitts, four bases, and a large outdoor area. Of course, you'll need other players, too—usually nine or ten to a side.

How it's Played

Formal softball games consist of seven rounds, called "innings." Each inning is separated into the top half and the bottom half. The visiting team gets to bat in the top half of the inning; the home team bats in the bottom half.

Each team continues to bat until its players make three outs. Only the batting team can score. The team with more points, or runs, at the end of seven innings wins the game. Sometimes, the home team is ahead after the visiting team bats in the top half of the final inning. When this is the case, there is no reason for the

People of any age and gender can enjoy softball.

home team to bat in the bottom half of the inning, so the game is over. If the score is tied after seven full innings, then extra innings may be played until a winner is determined. In extra innings, if the visiting team pulls ahead, the home team gets an opportunity in the bottom of the inning to tie the score or take the lead. The home team wins the game if it goes ahead in extra innings.

To end a game that is no longer competitive, some slow-pitch softball leagues use a "mercy rule." For example, if one team is beating the other by ten or twelve runs, the game is called off, and victory is awarded to the team that is far ahead. Usually, the rule is in effect only after the losing team has had at least three or four chances to bat.

Where it's Played

The exact size of a softball field can vary greatly, but the shape is always the same: four bases are set 60 feet apart (65 feet for slow-pitch), forming a diamond. Home plate is a five-sided slab of rubber that is 17 inches wide. First, second, and third bases are numbered counterclockwise and each is a 15 inch square. Lines extend from home plate toward first base and from home to third base. Known as foul lines, they extend past the bases into the outfield. They demarcate the foul territory (outside the lines) from the fair territory (inside the line).

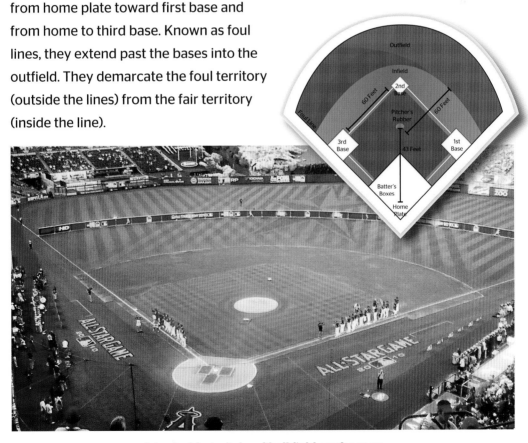

A typical fast-pitch softball field can be seen.

A "safety base" is mandatory in many leagues for safety reasons. This is a first base that is actually two bases, one of which sits in foul territory. To avoid collisions between the runner and the first baseman, the batter runs toward the foul base after hitting the ball. The defensive players use the "regular" base to try to get the runner out. For informal games, though, just about anything can be used for a base, such as a backpack or a jacket. The area enclosed by the bases and home plate comprises the infield; the area beyond the bases is known as the outfield. On many fields, a fence marks the outfield boundary.

Dugouts and Bullpens

Along each foul line, but safely behind it, is a dugout. The dugout is a long, narrow area for team members who are not on the field. At the higher levels of competition, dugouts often include equipment racks, water fountains, and telephones that call other parts of the ballpark. In public parks, a dugout might be just a wooden bench for players to sit on. Behind the dugout is the area where spectators can sit, whether that is a patch of grass or raised grandstands.

Finally, each team has a bullpen. These are designated areas outside the field of play where backup pitchers can throw practice pitches to get ready in case they are called into the game. Bullpens are usually either somewhere along the foul lines or beyond the outfield fence. Since there are no formal bullpens at public parks, pitchers prefer to warm up anywhere in foul territory that is out of harm's way.

On professional fields, dugouts often include amenities like storage space for equipment.

The bullpen provides the perfect space for practice just before a game.

Who Plays?

There are nine defensive players on the field at a time in many softball leagues, just like in baseball. The pitcher plays in the middle of the infield, and a catcher plays behind home plate. There are four other infielders. Near first base is the first baseman, and near third base is the third baseman. On the first-base side of second base is the second baseman, and on the third-base side is the shortstop. Three players patrol the outfield: the left fielder, the right fielder, and the center fielder. Some leagues allow a tenth fielder, who is usually positioned behind second base in the area known as short center field.

Uniforms and Equipment

All defensive players wear oversized, padded leather mitts that have webbing between the first finger and the thumb. The first baseman and catcher wear special mitts that have extra padding and no fingers. The catcher wears additional protection, including a wire mask and a padded chest protector. In fast-pitch leagues, catchers also wear hard plastic shin guards.

For league games, players on the same team all wear matching uniforms, which usually include caps and T-shirts or jerseys, and sometimes include matching pants. For informal games, sweats or other athletic clothing is good, but any comfortable clothes will do.

Batters wear protective helmets. All players should wear either sneakers or cleats. Cleats are special sneakers that have small spikes on their soles to provide better traction.

First basemen, like the one above, wear extra protection in the form of a helmet and a padded jersey.

Pitching

The pitcher must throw the ball through an imaginary rectangle above the home plate, called the "strike zone." Any pitch passing through the strike zone is considered hittable. The strike zone stretches from side to side above home plate. The exact boundaries of the strike zone depend on the batter; it usually extends from the batter's chest down to his or her knees.

Lisa Fernandez holds the Olympic record for twenty-five strikeouts in a game. Here, she is speaking at the closing ceremony of the Irvine Girls Softball Association in California, holding one of her Olympic medals.

Rules for Pitching

Softball players must make underhand throws, releasing the ball below their hip, regardless of whether the game is slow-pitched or fast-pitched. There are generally three types of slow-pitch softball. For regular slow-pitch, which is used in many recreational leagues, pitches must travel in an arc that peaks between 6 and 12 feet. In addition to regular slow-pitch, there are arc-pitch and modified slow-pitch. Pitches that peak higher than 12 feet above the ground are called arc-pitches.

All players must be alert on the pitch. The batter gets ready to swing the bat and the catcher gets ready to catch the ball.

Modified slow-pitch falls in between a fast-pitch and slow-pitch. The pitcher simply tosses the ball to the catcher in an underhand motion without attempting to put much speed or arc on the ball. Some slow pitchers can aim the ball very precisely. However, there is usually not a lot of strategy involved in the different types of slow pitching: the pitcher is simply trying to throw a hittable ball. Fast-pitch pitchers work very differently.

For fast-pitch softball, the distance between home plate and the pitching

rubber is 43 feet. The pitcher must throw the ball from within a circle with an eight-foot radius. Most fast-pitch pitchers start near the back of the circle and take a step or two toward home plate to give their pitches extra speed. They then whip their throwing arm around in a circular "windmill" motion before releasing the ball toward home plate.

Strategies for Pitching

The movements a pitcher makes while pitching are called "mechanics." Using proper mechanics helps a fast-pitch pitcher avoid injury while throwing hard. Proper mechanics also allow a pitcher to get power from his or her entire body instead of just the pitching arm. Coaches often play a large role in teaching good mechanics.

In order to prevent the batters from hitting the ball well, fast-pitch pitchers often employ various strategies. Pitch location is key, as pitches thrown to the edges and corners of the strike zone are more difficult to hit. Second, pitch speed is important. The faster a pitch is thrown, the less time the batter has to react and swing or decide not to swing. Finally, varying the pitch selection is key to keeping the batter off-balance. By gripping the ball differently or using different arm motions, the pitcher can pitch at different speeds or make the ball change direction in flight. Some common types of softball pitches are the fastball, change-up, curveball, riseball, and dropball.

Different types of pitchers excel at different aspects of pitching. "Power" pitchers can throw very hard; "control" pitchers have great accuracy; others are especially good at putting a lot of movement on their pitches. In competitive leagues, coaches will sometimes replace one type of pitcher with another at key points in a game to take advantage of a batter's weaknesses. But usually, a coach replaces a pitcher during a game because the pitcher is getting tired or is not pitching effectively.

The pitchers who begin the game are called "starting" pitchers. Pitchers who specialize in coming into a game that is already in progress are called "relief" pitchers. Though relief pitchers are very rare in slow-pitch softball, every college and world championship level team has at least one or two relief pitchers.

A player gets ready to pitch a softball.

Batting: Softball Offense

A batter stands in the batter's box, an area next to home plate, when he or she is "up" next. There is one such box on each side of the plate. Right-handed batters stand in the box on the left side of home plate, and lefties stand on the right side. The batter holds the bat handle with both hands, with his or her dominant (stronger) hand on top.

When a pitch is thrown, the batter decides whether to swing the bat. If the batter doesn't swing, an umpire must decide whether the pitch passed though the strike zone. If it did,

Hitting the ball as hard as possible gives the batter the chance to reach a base and not get out.

the pitch is called a "strike." It also counts as a strike if the batter swings at a pitch and misses it completely. Hitting a pitch into foul territory counts as a strike, as well. And, as the song says, it's "one, two, three strikes, you're out."

If the pitch did not pass through the strike zone, the umpire calls it a "ball." Four balls entitles the batter to a "walk," which is a free pass to first base.

A batter's main goal is to advance around the bases in order and return to home plate, scoring a run. A batter either reaches base or makes an out, and then the next batter gets a turn. Once on base, the batter becomes a runner. A hit that allows the batter to reach first base is called a single, getting to second base is a double, and to third base is a triple. Balls hit over the outfield fence in fair territory are home runs. A hit that stays in the park but allows the batter to circle the bases is called an inside-the-park home run.

Tips For Batting

- Don't be tense. Before each pitch, take a deep breath and exhale. Keep your hands relaxed right up to the moment you start your swing. Holding the bat too tightly takes away from your bat speed and control.

- The simplest and most common batting tip is to keep your eye on the ball all the way through your swing. When you hit the ball, you should be looking down the barrel of your bat, watching it make contact with the ball. Taking your eye off the ball may cause you to hit it foul or miss it completely.

- Follow through on your swing. This means continuing your swing, even after you hit the ball. Following through adds power to your swing and also helps prevent injury, especially if you miss the ball.

- Be patient and swing only at good pitches. It sounds simple, but swinging at good pitches may be the most important tip of all. Pitches that are outside the strike zone are difficult to hit. Don't help the opposition by swinging at pitches that would have been called balls.

- Keep your weight balanced on the balls of your feet, not on your heels. This will allow you to make quicker adjustments to the pitch. You will also get better plate coverage.

This batter waits patiently for the pitcher to pitch the ball so that she can make contact at the correct moment.

Fielding: Playing Defense

Every ball that the batter hits either goes down onto the ground (a ground ball or grounder) or up into the air (a fly ball). If a fielder catches a fly ball before it hits the ground, the batter is out. This is the rule even if the fly ball would have landed in foul territory.

The rules for ground balls are a little trickier. Once a fair ball touches the ground, there are two ways to get the batter out. First, a fielder can tag the batter with the ball while the batter is not touching any base. Or, a fielder can touch first base while holding the ball before the batter gets there. The first baseman is usually the one who does that. The main job of the other infielders is to scoop up ground balls and throw them to the first baseman before the batter gets there. Infielders also catch line drives and short fly balls that don't make it all the way to the outfield.

Proper technique fielding ground balls helps insure that the ball doesn't get past the fielder and yield extra bases to the runner.

Outfielders catch fly balls for outs. However, for ground balls that get through the infield, it's usually impossible to get the batter out at first base. If the batter tries to advance to second base or beyond, then the outfielders try to throw the ball to the infielder who can tag the batter out. If two runners get out on one play, it is called a double play. Getting three players out on one play, which is very rare, is called a triple play.

How to Catch Flies

Judging how far a fly ball will travel and where you need to go in order to catch it requires a lot of practice. The more fly balls you see as a fielder, the better you'll be at judging them, and the quicker you'll be able to get to the right spot. The best way to practice is to have someone throw or hit fly balls to you over and over again.

Many inexperienced players tend to run after fly balls with their arms up in the air. But doing that slows you down and makes it harder to adjust if you need to. You can move a lot faster if you wait until you're in position and then raise your glove for the catch.

The best way to catch a fly ball is to keep practicing to improve your judgement.

Rules for Grounders

If you can't field a ground ball cleanly, the most important thing you can do is to knock it down and keep it in front of you. This will keep any base runner from advancing further. Proper positioning helps keep the ball from getting past you. Getting your whole body—not just your mitt—directly in the path of the ball puts you in a better position to react if the ball takes a tricky bounce. Outfielders, especially, need to make sure that the ball doesn't get past them. (There's nobody behind them to back them up.) For an outfielder, the best approach is usually to get down on one knee, so that your body will block the ball if it misses your glove.

Infielders are in a much bigger hurry, though. They have to scoop up the ball and throw it to first base before the runner gets there. As an infielder, you should stay on your feet whenever possible, but still try to get your body in front of the ball. You should also make sure to bend your knees, keeping your back straight. This way, instead of looking down at the ground, you can look straight ahead at the ball. If the ground ball is below your waist, turn your glove in such a way that your fingers point to the ground. Watch the ball all the way, and use your bare hand to secure the ball once it hits your glove.

First Catch, Then Throw

One common mistake by fielders in all positions is thinking about what to do with the ball before it's actually in your glove. You can't throw what you don't have, so make sure you watch the ball go into your glove before you try to do anything with it.

The Difference Between Softball and Baseball

Softballs and baseballs are constructed the same way. They both have a core made of rubber or rubber and cork. This core is wrapped in layers of tightly wound string or yarn and covered with stitched leather. The main difference is that the yarn in softballs is wound with less tension than a baseball. This means that a softball will not travel as far as a baseball hit with the same force.

In addition to being played with different balls, baseball and softball also have different bats. The barrel of a softball bat—the wide part of the bat that strikes the ball—is longer than the barrel of a baseball bat, providing a bigger "sweet spot." The differences in the bats are a direct result of the differences in the ball. Because baseballs can travel farther than softballs, baseball bats are designed to help the batter hit the ball as hard and as far as possible. In softball, on the other hand, hit placement is often more important than distance. This is why softball bats are designed to give the hitter more command of where the ball goes and better bat control.

Though the rules of both softball and baseball are almost identical, the equipment and pitching techniques used, differ.

CHAPTER 3

Strategy and Rules

Softball and baseball have the same basic rules, except for a few key differences. Specific softball rules may change depending on the level of competition.

The Umpire

No matter the level of play, the umpires are in charge. Umpires are impartial judges who watch the action on the field, enforce the rules of the game, and have the final say on all questions and disputes. The number of umpires on the field varies depending on the league and level of play. Some leagues can have a single umpire and some can have as many as six.

The umpire stands behind the catcher so that he can see each pitch clearly. He ducks while the pitch is being thrown to avoid getting hit.

A specific job is given to each umpire. The home plate umpire, who calls balls and strikes, stands behind the catcher to get the best view of every pitch. Like the catcher, the home plate umpire wears a protective mask and chest pad.

Base umpires stand near the bases and decide whether a runner is safe or out, and also call whether a batted ball is fair or foul. If there is only one umpire present, he or she stands behind the pitcher to be able to see as much of the field as possible. Most fast-pitch games are called by a crew of two umpires. One stands behind home plate, calling balls and strikes and foul balls, and the other umpire stands near second base, making most other calls. Umpires are often called by the nickname "Blue" because of the color of most umpire uniforms.

Strategy and Managing

Every competitive softball team has a manager; teams may also have coaches. The manager's job varies depending on the level of competition. The manager's general duties involve determining game strategy, organizing team practices, giving instructions, setting the batting order for each team, and determining who plays the field and when.

Strategy and team coordination are an important part of a softball game.

The Batting Order

The lineup, or batting order, cannot change throughout the game, which is why a lot of thought and strategy goes behind making it. In general, the better hitters go toward the top of the batting order. The first batter in the order is called the leadoff hitter. He

by ejendals

The batter has just hit the ball and is ready to run to first base.

or she is usually fast runner who is good at getting on base. Usually, the second hitter is also speedy. The team's best hitter usually bats third. The idea is that the first two hitters get on base so that the third hitter can drive them in with a hit. The most powerful hitter usually bats fourth, in the "clean-up" spot. It is so called because the team hopes the fourth hitter will clear all the runners off the bases with a home run. If the first four batters all do their jobs, the score is already 4–0 by the time the fifth batter comes up to plate. The game rarely works out exactly that way, but this is the most commonly used strategy in setting a batting order.

The manager also handles all player substitutions. This can be a tricky job because, unlike most other sports, players who come out of a game are not allowed back in. The substitute must bat in the exact same spot as the player he is replacing.

Most teams enjoy a pre-game pep talk where strategy is discussed.

Coaches often specialize in either pitching or hitting, and sometimes even double as base coaches. Base coaches stand in foul territory outside first and third bases, telling runners when it's safe to run to the next base. They also use hand signals to give advice to batters and base runners. Before each pitch, the third–base coach shows the batter a sequence of hand signs designed to convey secret instructions without letting the other team know what to expect. The coach usually gets those instructions from the manager.

One of the common instructions tells the batter to bunt. For a bunt, the batter attempts to hit the ball gently by simply sticking the bat out in the path of the ball instead of swinging the bat through the strike zone. The goal is to make the ball roll slowly a short distance and then stop, making the fielders run from their normal positions to pick it up. This often gives the batter enough time to reach first base safely. Another reason to bunt is to advance a runner who is already on base. These bunts are called "sacrifices" because the batter helps his or her team move the runner to the next base by intentionally making an out.

Coaches are instrumental in the performance of their team. Here, a coach takes care of an injured player.

Baserunning

Sometimes, when a batter hits a ground ball and runs to first base, there is a already a player on first base. In such cases, that runner has to make room for the batter by running to second base. He or she is "forced" to run. If another runner is already occupying second base, that runner has to make room by going to third, and so on. The same carousel is set in motion if a batter walks, although all the runners get a pass to the next base.

This player makes a dash for the second base.

If a batter hits a ground ball when there is a runner on second or third base only, the runner on base may choose to advance if it's safe to do so, though he or she is not forced to go.

Braden Scott, a Canadian softball player, slides towards second base, attempting to touch the base before the fielder tags him.

If a runner is forced to run to the next base by a batter or runner behind him, then he need not be tagged by the ball to get out. The fielder can simply touch or step on the base the runner is trying to reach to get him or her out. That is called a force out. But a runner who is not being forced to advance to the next base by someone running behind him or her, can only be put out with a tag.

Force play usually occurs at first base. A batter who drives a ball on the ground into fair territory must run to first base. If a defensive player fields the ball and throws it to first base (that is, to a fielder who is touching first base while catching the ball) before the batter can reach it, the batter is out.

When the batter hits a ground ball, runners can move up even if they're not forced, but fly balls work a bit differently. If a runner leaves his or her base before a fly ball is caught, the runner must return to the base. If a fielder with the ball can step on the base before the runner gets back, the runner is out—double play. However, if the runner stays on the base until the fly ball is caught, he or she may remain safely on the base or try to advance.

Tagging Up and Stealing

In fast-pitch softball, a runner may try to advance to the next base at any time. However, because of the risk of being tagged out, the runner usually waits until the batter hits the ball before running for the next base. "Stealing" a base means that the runner tries running to the next base while the pitcher is in the act of pitching the ball. If the runner is not quick enough, the play can backfire. The catcher can throw the ball to the player guarding the next base, who can tag the runner out.

This player has just pitched a ball.

In addition to stealing bases and running on a hit, runners can try to advance after a fly ball has been caught or when a fielder makes an error. If you advance after a fly ball has been caught, it is called "tagging up."

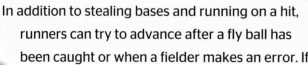

This fielder is trying to catch a fly ball in
an attempt to get the better out.

CHAPTER 4

Getting Involved

You can buy softball equipment from any sporting goods store. If you don't live near a store, there are dozens of general sporting goods web sites, plus several that specialize in gloves, bats, and balls.

Playing With the Right Equipment

If you're looking for equipment to get started, the first thing you'll need is a mitt. Players are usually happy to let others use their bats and balls, but they can be protective of their mitts, so you'll probably need your own.

Each player has their own pair of mitts.

A baseball mitt will be fine, but if you're buying a new mitt, choose one that's made specifically for softball (they're usually labeled). The gloves for each position are also slightly different, so it's a good idea for you to know whether you want to play in the infield or the outfield. Outfielders have slightly larger gloves to help them catch fly balls and to prevent those fly balls from bouncing out of the glove. Infielders' gloves are a bit smaller to make it easier to get the ball out quickly. It's best to store your new mitt with a softball tucked inside, to help shape it.

Buying a bat can be confusing, with so many sizes, weights, and different types of aluminum. In general, stronger players should use bigger, heavier bats, and smaller players should use smaller bats. Get a bat made specifically for softball—most softball leagues don't allow baseball bats. For length, a good rule of thumb is to use a bat that comes up to your waist when standing on end. Another way to choose a bat of the right length is to find one that reaches just past the far side of home plate when you swing. Keep in mind that softball bats longer than 34 inches are not allowed.

The weight of a bat generally goes down or up in relation to its length, so once you decide on a length, the choices for weight will

Softball bats are of various sizes and types. You need to find the size that suits you best for optimal results.

be limited. Heavier bats provide more power, but lighter bats give you more control and a faster swing, which also helps your power.

There are a plethora of other supplies and training devices available in the market, from batting gloves to doughnut-shaped bat weights, but there is no substitute for a good glove and a good bat if you want to get ahead in the game.

Start Playing

Having all the equipment is pointless if you aren't going to get into a game. You might already know of a regular weekend pick-up game in your town. If not, you can check out local parks. Another great place to start is your local Little League.

Founded in 1939, Little League organizes baseball and fast-pitch softball teams for boys and girls between the ages of five and eighteen. Local leagues typically have several divisions based mostly on age and partly on skill. Little League has thousands of chapters in the United States, so chances are there's a league not far from where you live.

There are thousands of Little League chapters across the United States.

Babe Ruth League is another option. Depending on what part of the country you live in, there is softball for girls ages five to eighteen, in a league structure very similar to Little League. If neither league has a team nearby, you can contact the leagues' national headquarters to inquire about starting one. Or, you can ask about other local leagues organized through schools or houses of worship. Another option for improving your game is to attend one of the many softball camps and clinics held throughout the United States. Former players and coaches usually organize them.

Playing Safely

The primary concern of all these organizations is safety. Despite its name, softball can be a dangerous game. Batters and catchers must wear the appropriate protective gear at all times, and players should be careful to check who is around before swinging bats or throwing balls. Even with all the standard protection, softball is a sport like any other, and injuries happen. The best way to be safe is to do some simple stretching before games and practices to get your muscles loose. During practices and games, stay alert. If you're paying attention to the game, you won't be caught off-guard by a ball or another player flying your way.

Practicing

If you make a team, you can expect to practice on days in between games. At a typical practice for a school or youth league team, one team member will bat while the others play the field, and after a few minutes, the batter heads out to the field and someone else takes a turn at bat. This way, everyone on the team gets a chance to practice hitting, and everyone gets to work on fielding, too. Coaches take direct fielding and running drills after batting practice, to observe your technique and give you advice for improving your game.

Professional players practice batting and fielding daily.

Exiting The Olympics

Softball was last played at the Olympics at the 2008 Summer Games in Beijing, China. In July 2005, members of the International Olympic Committee (IOC) voted to drop baseball and softball from the 2012 Games. In spite of protests from around the world, the IOC confirmed its decision in another vote in February 2006. It was decided that the sport would be left out of the 2016 Olympics too. On September 8th, 2013, the IOC had to vote for the reinstatement of one dropped Olympic sport. Though baseball-softball was a strong contender, it lost to wrestling, which will now be included in the 2020 and 2024 Olympics.

The Australian women's softball team parades in Sydney after the Beijing Olympics in 2008. This was the last time this game was played at the Olympics.

Softball fans all over the world are upset about the snub, most notably International Softball Federation president Don Porter. "The end result is that thousands and thousands of young female athletes effectively have their Olympic dreams fading away," Porter said.

The Season

Unless you live in a climate that allows for outdoor play all year round, softball is usually played only in the spring and summer. School leagues and Little League schedules tend to start in early spring and finish by the time school lets out for summer. If you live in an area where the sport is popular, you might be able to find summer youth leagues, too.

At the end of the season, most leagues have a series of play-offs between the top teams to determine a league champion. The top teams are determined simply by who wins the most games during the regular season.

Winning the Game

Many leagues and schools have a national play-off system. Little League, for example, has each local league send a team of all-stars to district competition. Winners continue playing for divisional and then regional titles. The American regional winners and champions from other countries then compete in the nationally televised Little League World Series. This tournament is held every August at Alpenrose Field in Portland, Oregon. In high school leagues, teams that have the best record usually play in a city or county tournament, with the winner moving on to the state and then national championships.

At the college level, the National College Athletic Association (NCAA) oversees three skill-based divisions, each with its own championship. School teams in the top division compete to earn a trip to the College Softball World Series.

In Little League and the NCAA, softball is open only to female players, but there are many championships for men as well. A men's world championship for fast-pitch and a separate world championship for slow-pitch are held every year, as are junior men's and women's world championships.

The World Cup of Softball is a tournament that is held annually at the ASA Hall of Fame Stadium in Oklahoma City, Oklahoma.

A batter for the Drama Killers team prepares to hit a ball in a game against the Outkast team in the Co-ed Softball League.

Softball is one of the few sports that is popular enough to support women's fast-pitch professional leagues. The top professional league is the National Pro Fast-pitch Softball League, which drafts college players every year and includes several stars from past Olympic teams. The league has seven teams and a forty-eight-game schedule, and has held a championship game every year since 1997. If you are passionate enough and willing to work hard, who knows, some day you might be a pro player too!

Monica Abbot participated in the 2008 Beijing Olympics,
in which the U.S. women's softball team won the silver medal.

Glossary

alumni Graduates or former students of a school, college, or university. (The plural form of alumnus.)

amateur In sports, a nonprofessional.

arc An arch or curve, as in the flight of a pitched ball.

bunt A hitting tactic used in baseball and softball. For a bunt, the batter turns to face the pitcher and holds the bat in the path of the ball so that the ball travels only a short distance when hit.

circumference The distance around circle or sphere.

double play A play in baseball or softball in which the defensive team puts out two players from the hitting team.

exhibition A public demonstration or showing.

grandstands Seating for spectators.

heckle To embarrass or annoy with insults or gestures.

high jinks Carefree antics or horseplay.

impartial Treating all equally.

perfect game A no-hitter in which a pitcher pitches the entire game without a single batter from the opposing team reaching base by any method, such as a walk or error.

pick-up game An informal game that can be joined by anyone who happens to be on or near the field at the time.

recreational Done for fun or diversion.

vacant Not occupied or put to use.

For More Information

Organizations

Amateur Softball Association of America (ASA)
2801 NE 50th Street
Oklahoma City, OK 73111
(405) 424-5266
Web site: http://www.asasoftball.com

Babe Ruth League
1770 Brunswick Pike,
P.O. Box 5000
Trenton, NJ 08638
(609) 695-1434
Web site: http://www.baberuthleague.org

Independent Softball Association
680 East Main Street
Suite 101
Bartow, FL 33830
(863) 533-4290
Web site: http://www.isasoftball.com

International Softball Federation
1900 S. Park Road
Plant City, FL 33563
(813) 864-0100
Web site: http://www.isfsoftball.org

Little League International Baseball and Softball
539 U.S. Route 15 Hwy
P.O. Box 3485
Williamsport, PA 17701-0485
(570) 326-1921
Web site: http://www.littleleague.org

National Collegiate Athletics Association (NCAA)
700 W. Washington Street
P.O. Box 6222
Indianapolis, IN 46206-6222
(317) 917-6222
Web site: http://www.ncaa.org

National Pro Fastpitch (NPF)
3350 Hobson Pike
Hermitage, TN 37076
(615) 232-8880
Web site: http://profastpitch.com

United States Fastpitch Association (USFA)
22912 Ann Miller Road
Panama City Beach, FL 32413
(850) 234-2839
Web site: http://www.usfastpitch.com

Magazines

Softball Magazine
411 Magnolia Avenue
Merritt Island, FL 32952-4821
(321) 453-3711
Web site: http://www.softballmag.com

Softball Today Magazine
5663 Balboa Ave., #372
San Diego, CA 92111
(858) 715-9280
Web site: http://www.softballtoday.com

World Softball Magazine
International Softball Federation
1900 S. Park Road
Plant City, FL 33563
(813) 864 0100
Web site: http://www.isfsoftball.org/english/communication/magazine.asp

Web Sites

Due to the changing nature of Internet links, Rosen Publishing Group, has developed an online list of Web sites related to the subject of this book. This site is updated regularly. Please use this link to access the list:

http://www.rosenlinks.com/STTS/Soft

For Further Reading

Finch, Jennie. *Throw Like a Girl: How to Dream Big and Believe in Yourself*. Chicago, IL: Triumph Books, 2011.

Garman, Judi, and Michelle Gromacki. *Softball Skills & Drills*. Champaign, IL: Human Kinetics, 2011.

Gola, Mark. *Winning Softball for Girls*. New York, NY: Chelsea House, 2009.

Martens, Rainer, and Julie Martens. *Complete Guide to Slowpitch Softball*. Champaign, IL: Human Kinetics, 2007.

Potter, Diane and Lynn Johnson. *Softball: Steps to Success*. Champaign, IL: Human Kinetics, 2007.

Smith, Michele, and Lawrence Hsieh. *Coach's Guide to Game-Winning Softball Drills: Developing the Essential Skills in Every Player*. Camden, ME: International Marine/McGraw-Hill, 2008.

Schwartz, Heather E. *Winning on the Diamond*. North Mankato, MN: Capstone, 2007.

Walker, Kirk. *The Softball Drill Book*. Champaign, IL: Human Kinetics, 2007.

Weekly, Ralph, and Karen Weekly. *High-Scoring Softball*. Champaign, IL: Human Kinetics, 2012.

Bibliography

Bealle, Morris A. *The Softball Story: A Complete, Concise and Entertaining History of America's Greatest Participant and Spectator Sport.* New York, NY: Columbia, 1957.

Dickson, Paul. *The Worth Book of Softball: A Celebration of America's True National Pastime.* New York, NY: Facts on File, 1994.

International Softball Federation. "The History of Softball." Retrieved January 26, 2006 (http://www.internationalsoftball.com/english/the_isf/history_of_softball.asp).

Joseph, Jacqueline. *The Softball Coaching Bible.* Champaign, IL: Human Kinetics, 2002.

The King and His Court. "It All Started on a Dare." 2003. Retrieved February 21, 2006 (http://www.kingandhiscourt.com).

Strahan, Kathy. *Coaching Girls' Softball: From the How-To's of the Game to Practical Real-World Advice.* Roseville, CA: Prima, 2001.

Index

About the Authors

Jayne Baker is a writer based in Oklahoma City, Oklahoma, which has been dubbed the "Softball Capital of the World."

Adam B. Hofstetter has written about sports for SportsIllustrated.com and other publications. He is an avid softball player and can often be found on the various softball fields of New York, where he lives with his wife and two children.

Photo Credits